BEACONS, BLUES AND HOLY GOATS

For Margaret.

With gratitude, wishing
you peace, wonder and wellness
for the journey.

Stephen T. Brug

BEACONS,
BLUES
and
HOLY GOATS

Stephen T Berg

Aeolus House

Author Photo: Stephen T Berg
Cover Design and Typography: McNeill Design Arts
Editor: Allan Briesmaster

Library and Archives Canada Cataloguing in Publication

Title: Beacons, blues and holy goats / Stephen T. Berg.
Names: Berg, Stephen T., 1954- author.
Identifiers: Canadiana 20190135328 | ISBN 9781987872194 (softcover)
Classification: LCC PS8603.E67515 B43 2019 | DDC C811/.6—dc23

Published by
Aeolus House
an imprint of Quattro Books Inc.
P.O. Box 53031
Royal Orchard Postal Station
10 Royal Orchard Blvd.
Thornhill, ON L3T 3C0
www.aeolushouse.com

Printed in Canada

For my mother and father, now gone, still here.

We must risk delight. We can do without pleasure,
but not delight. Not enjoyment. We must have
the stubbornness to accept our gladness in the ruthless
furnace of the world.

                    – Jack Gilbert, "A Brief for the Defence"

Contents

HOLY GOATS

Poem Broken Open

I like the ribald poems of sloggers and shufflers, their sweeping hands and glint-eyes, the meat still in their teeth as they tell it loud.

I like swaggering poems – poems that have a pack of Players rolled up under a short-sleeve. I like bawdy, libidinous, flowing, flowering Song of Solomon poems;

I like a full-lipped-Flaubert of a poem. And I like the balanced elegance of plaited verse – a filigree of Frost.

I like a surprise lyric – one that at the end of a perfect day happily pushes you in the pool. And I love the one that steals you away to a slow river with broad grassy banks, and lets you lie there and breathe.

Such permission in a poem is like roughed-in plumbing – all you need do is choose your tub, fill and bathe.

I like poems that are unsure of themselves. An educator will say these are weak and deficient, but I like them because they are so much like people.

I like a carefully-wrapped haiku, and inside something turquoise and without purpose – but for its *old pond* beauty.

I like care-less poems, poems that sleep-in, then leave you notes under your windshield wiper while you're in church – telling you when and where to meet them.

I love a free-verse small epiphany poem – like a friend skipping class that hangs outside your schoolroom window madly waving her arms and grinning, waiting for you to notice her – and the clear sky behind.

I like the ones that take you seriously, respect your mind and your time – and if not your time, at least your mind.

But I don't like freighted teleological poems or big cosmic ontological poems. They are like model rockets – all decals and plastic – that topple over in a minor gust, spark and fizzle and spin in circles on the pavement.

Don't like poems that tousle you, hated being tousled, hate the word *tousle*.

And I don't much like hail-fellow-well-met cowboy poems, although I'll admit to smiling every time.

Don't like high-flown, God-bless-'em poems. They're all doily. They don't have ears. So how can they have a heart?

I do not care for a poem that supports a thesis, unless it came before the thesis was conceived, in which case it can glow – prescient in brilliance.

More, I like poems that spitball you, chase you and chide you with their slant rhymes and bumpy meter and screwy trochee – and you sit there and take it because they're saying something important.

But the poem that breaks me open, the one that hurts without doing me harm, oh, give me this:

Give me your signet, your sonnet, your elegy or epic, and I'll climb, kneel, open my hands, eat the host and drink the wine; trust me, I'd wait through any black night with you.

BEACONS

Dallas Road Cliffs

The Dallas Road cliffs cast echoes of light
across a softening percussion of waves.

The day is dying
and people are leaving
for the listing boats of sleep.

Consenting to your fading horizon,
you stay in place, waiting
on the slow birds of night.

Still, how beautiful the next breath,
how liberating this unhurried hour,
how surprising the extempore prayer –

how crucial, the unbidden poem,
like a sacred friend,
who names your sorrow,
fills the hollows with hope,
beacons out a gentle way.

Walking a Fence Line North of Chip Lake

I saw a vision of my dad
standing on a stony rise,
like the one in Saskatchewan
on the west side of the Riverside Farm.
I saw his left hand lift, and in one fluid pass
remove a green and white Co-op cap, draw
forearm across brow and replace the cap.
Some thick black hair escaped and curled up
past a sweat-greyed brim. Beneath
a grease-stained bill, even at that distance,
his famous robin's-egg blue eyes glistened.
He turned toward me as though to speak,
his mouth opened and I heard the wind
take away what it was he was moved to say.

Yesterday, walking the slopes in that visible heat,
with last year's stubble breaking beneath my boots,
white cockle and quackgrass bristling on the crests,
I thought I saw our old yellow Chevy half-ton
parked by the fallen fence behind the yard,
almost lost in the grass. Then the tailgate was down
and we were eating lunch. Between us
was a quart jar of tea wrapped in a dish towel.
We ate with dirt-creased fingers
making prints in white-bread sandwiches.

I watched the terns, their sickle wings
reaping the air, making low swoops, plucking grubs
from fresh-turned soil behind the seeder.
Dad looked past them to the horizon.

I knew at times the land frustrated him.
He buried himself in it but his love wasn't total.
There was another world in him, hinted at, but not spoken.

How is it that more than forty years later, and my father gone
these twenty, I sit in a field of silent questions,
waiting for a sprout of answers?

Were you proud of me then? Did you understand
the confusion I couldn't shake?
Did you forgive my leaving?

I know I was proud of you.
When island pub-talk turned, as it always did, to telling
prairie histories, I listed your careers, initiatives,
positions, your life of crop rotations, some successful.
Now I just miss the grace of sitting in that space
between the empty jar of tea and the belch of tractor engine,
the truck radio tuned to CJGX: weather forecast, grain exchange,
farm report, aimed out the window and lost in the fallow.

I remember the year when time got away from you
and the north quarter grew wild past cultivating –
until summer, when it was cut, swathed,
burned and turned under as one does to a mistake.
Your blunder was held up in town at the coffee shop.
But I recall some small thing you said,
and a slight smile that following fall,
when the harvest there was better than average.

Come down from the rise. I want to sit on the tailgate
and talk about the way of things. How I learned from you
to plough under my annual crop of rank mistakes,
pray for timely rains and hope for a good harvest.

Come down from that silent slope, I want
to hear those words that were lost in the wind.

Recorded in a Haze of Aspen Saplings

Above the cliffs along the Juan de Fuca strait are fragments of prairie,
and when I walk dutifully on the asphalt paths
beside the meadow barley, nodding onion and Nootka rose,
I nod to the spirits within,
in recognition
of a bone-deep bond
with the grasses, forbs and shrubs that still green my prairie blood,
where as a boy I ran,
arms outstretched through shoulder-high wild rye.

I was called into the silver tunnels of willow and buffaloberry,
knelt as one knighted at the Indigo Milk Caps,
sailed a scrap-lumber frigate held fast by spike and rope
through battalions of bullrush,
their velvet heads bursting up small clouds of down.
Coyotes held my head above sleep in windless nights
and tri-toned trains poured poems into sedge-lined skylines.

My birth is recorded in a haze of aspen saplings
on the crest of the Whitesand River,
where swallows of mercy inhabit a mud-chinked log house
that stands as a cenotaph
to the plowers and mothers and hard long hours,
where windrows of scrub brush burned far into winter,
where coulter and ploughshare,
cut sod, bled summerfallow,
and bouts of drought and blankets of hail
gave way to a red barn, white chickens and bins of barley,
where a pine-trimmed house
saw the coming and parting of five children, all
dreaming of voyages beyond the bush-belted yard
where now, through some trick of time, I walk
among the joyful spirits of goldenrod, blue stem and sagebrush,
listening to the drumming angels of the great plains,
aflame with a desire I can't name,
and happy for it.

August Mushrooms Brought on by July Rains

Forget fungal colonies
    growing on nutrient-rich agar plates.
Lean low with your camera, knees in dirt and dead leaves, and capture
    this bit of wonder:
    August mushrooms brought on by July rains.
Fruiting bodies erupt from the soil,
    round caps push up through layer-cake loam,
    small mounds of desire.
Notice the full hips, the botox-smooth brow, the parted fluting beneath,
    and the salt-air smell of spore and earth, the effulgence of fungi,
    the sexual and asexual mystery of mushrooms,
    waiting for replication from within,
    waiting to burst into the thick air to be taken afield or abroad,
Garishly flocculent, sometimes tasty, yet within there's a galactic secret:
    a mat of micro-threads,
    a network of hyphae crossing the earth's continents and oceans.
Imagine the planet,
    sentient.
Imagine the earth,
    a dolphin swimming in an ethereal yet viscous vacuum.
Imagine the rain forest, great lungs oxygenating the wild blue currents of air,
    giving strength to the wind and gathering rains that break open,
    run over the greening soil
    and back into the capillaries and veins that return to the sea.
Imagine the sea a heart,
    its cleansing and constant beating tides raising vast blankets of brume
    that dewily sink and settle upon soft ground.
And imagine the ground, the loam and loess,
    as that sleek dark-grey body hosting a sensorial instrument,
    alive and intricate and capable of an intelligence
    beyond our tool-oriented intellect.
It is this skin, this vegetative part of fungi, the out-of-sight mycelium mat
    living in the top six inches of most of the globe's soil, that,
    while outside of our powers of comprehension,
    may yet save us from the wounds we've cut into the earth.
Here on this slip of turf, I crouch by the amanita muscaria that has sprung up
    from the earth's blanket, bewitching, alluring, poisonous, but rarely fatal.
    Its growth, connected to an amanita in Argentina,
    a morel in Morocco, a porcini in Italy,
    its genome, joined, allied to our own.

Black Turnstones

When you return to me on some new day,
we'll walk to the cliffs then descend to the shore.
And when I point out the Black Turnstones
picking their way along the wave-washed rocks,
searching for acorn barnacles and corded limpets,
we'll cheer to see their humble sandpiper bodies
insinuating themselves, monk-like,
into the jagged cloisters of their granite abbeys.
Wait 'til they take flight, you'll say, and we'll wait
and they'll lift in quick chorus, and we'll trace,
in the scapular flair of their wings,
the whirring utterance of *amen*,
a declaration of divinity,
patterned against the green-slate sea.
We'll talk, then, of their untaught faith
in finding, daily, what is needed for strength.
We'll note their belief in original goodness,
their simple trust in the grace of littoral space.
And we'll pause too, won't we? at some twinkling tide pool,
some gentle rivulet running over basalt,
some gleaming sea star,
some reflective stillness on sun-glazed sandstone,
some intrepid sea palm swaying in the psalm of heavy surf,
open to connection, open to communion, open to conversion,
the *ora et labora* of this botanical beach.
And won't we rise to what feels like a fanning
of our own courage in the glide and dive
of a double-crested cormorant?
Won't we be delivered?
Won't our hearts grow deliciously wild?

Deer in a Clearing

When she sees me her ears go up like small rocket ships
and her nose lifts to sip the air.
Her body is wind and spring steel,
the still deep oscillation of tension and release.

When I move, I am a plough lurching over hardpan,
I am an oaf of the meadow, I am
that slumping bale of hay by the bush.
Unfit for this scene, a passing curiosity,
a bit of humour in the day, for the deer.

But I stop, stand *stabilitas* still,
and she gives me this:

When I move diagonally,
she steps carefully after me –
light glancing off hooves held high,
her legs like thin articulated silhouettes.

When I turn, she turns,
jumps twice, stops, swings back,
pivots perfectly to face me again.

She suffers my plodding dance
but I will dance like this as long as she wants –
for her intelligence is of some new world,
where silence and flowers bestow meaning
and *truth springs out of the earth.*

She lives beyond the thing within the thing itself,
knows the touch of autumn in the smell of tansy,
feels the wind when the wind's mind thinks to move,
lives at the break of clover, at the budding of dawn,
sees the fall of empires in the sweet-pea's keeled bloom,
while I stand knee-deep in this grass,
                    dim to its feathery glumes.

Grey Burnaby Day

What we have here is a grey Burnaby day,
that could well be a grey day anywhere in the world.
What we have here are great heaps of mist and cloud
that could stand in for all the sorrow in the world.

And rain –
rain that weeps from eyes the size of continents
on ground already wet by weeks.
Rain, that leaves your last happy memory,
once blithely stored for such a day,
to leach away behind your leaden eyes.

Not unlike all the leaden eyes in this long line of bipeds
who come to this coffee shop,
its awning the colour of mould,
to put off the manacled moment
when they snatch up their mildewing umbrellas
and ride a train to their purposeless jobs, longing
for lives not their own, even some neighbour's nostalgia.

And with your mind tamped down like gunpowder
into the barrel of this morning-born-old,
you think to rise as though to shout:
This is how emptiness feels. And if you haven't noticed,
meaning has left on the last sky-train,
cackling its fucking incoherence.

But who knows how these things work?
Who knows how the trip and pitch of angular seconds
tick at the access and egress of some nick-in-time,
kick at the coals of some dying star,
to spark alive the human locomotive.

Because what we have here is a barista who stops the line,
moves from behind her counter to carry the cup
of a woman wending her walker through the door
to take her place on the patio.

And what we have is a young man wearing a bright-blue bandana
who leaves his place under the awning, retrieves a napkin,
wipes spittle and spill from the shirtfront
of a man in a wheelchair with candle-flame eyes.

What we have here are hands ensouled and flesh-robed grace,
in the embrace of friends meeting before a long parting,
in some soul by the window who smiles without looking up
at the glory of this thin space, with a street address,
and postal code, that is like anywhere in the world,
open to the deep mists and the holy grey rain of a winter day.

Ungoverned

A young woman in a one-button Burberry blazer crowds the plodding man.
Coffee and impatience in hand, she insinuates him through the exit into the
    street.

The old man is aware but his gait is staid – like he's walked this way all his life.
He is wishing himself quicker for the sake of the woman – he has no quarrel.

He is bound to nothing more urgent than the earth's rotation.
He has the walk of the ungoverned – slow enough for anyone to catch on.

He has learned not to pile his hair high and worry its descent.
He is quizzical but not fascinated by technique. He is unmoved by Apple.

His domain is boulevards with begonias and parks with birdbaths,
coffee shops with patios and pubs with Blue Buck on tap.

He is comfortable with pickers and panhandlers but could easily fledge
    among the heeled
without the preening self-consciousness of the Birkin-possessed.

Neither habit-hobbled nor entirely untethered, he is a friend of the magpie,
and only slightly jealous of the bird of Juno.

Grain Elevator Scene Circa 1979

Leftover light from a harvest moon
lies on ice crust in frozen ruts   Trucks
line up at the open bay doors   Light
the colour of puffed-wheat sifts morning
through the breezeway   Grain elevators –
Pioneer red, Pool green, Federal white
– tower over train tracks worn silver
by steel wheels   Sun-soaked railroad ties, funk
of creosote in swirls of barley
Dust rising from a grain spout   Weeds sprout
out of a hill of spilled oilseed
Mouse runs beneath rind of red clover
and green mats of germinated oats
Knots of quackgrass and thistle between
spur line and trunk line and swing-nose switch
Euclidean line of Canada
Wheat Board hopper cars along annex
recedes to cottonwood horizons
Come-along winch bites spooled sisal rope
Rope strains at the tonnage of train, *Watch*
you don't lose a leg to her, son, I
had a friend ...   Rusted boxcars coopered
with corrugated paperboard and spring
-steel straps   Claw hammer hangs on unplaned
one-by-six   Flex spout flings Bonanza
barley to the car's far end from a
100-foot leg running up the cribbed
walls to the cupola, terminus
of rope-pull man-lift with deadman brake,
where wood troughs at bin tops wear lacquer
smooth, a lustered relief by Red Spring
Wheat, and my boss, Lorne Harrison, says,
Now that's art, son; but it's all art, son.
Buying grain is all about beauty –
every kernel, translucent glory.

Garden Trowel

Here where the Holy Bible,
gilded as Solomon, lies
prostrate on the pulpit,
smooth hands rise and fall,
tracing a trident sermon:
Snake cunning!
Eve prostrate!
Church militant!
And the faithful rise
to hurl mountains into seas,
and the newborn righteous
rattle verses over the heads
of the condemned, who
come fiercely forward,
confessing bright nights
and lazy afternoons
and morning erections
of craven monuments.

And you sit in your pew,
your irresolute head turned to the window
and recall the way your woman wears
her jeans to bed and nothing else
enlists your concupiscent mind,
but for the sun's light falling
outside, on a half-open leaf,
and her watercolour hand,
holding a garden trowel,
palm up, fingers curled
loose and lingering,
the way she bends
at the waist over
tomato plants.
And you feel
the smile
of God.

Birthday Sonnet
for D

I cannot say as much as the butterfly,
I do not speak Nymphalidae,
and I cannot pupate these promissory
words into a silver-washed fritillary.
But on this, your 55th circuit of sun, I still
crave to cocoon with you, still thrill
at the sight of you. Blessed by our leaf-shade
love in the leaden heat of a dogged day.
Blessed this love spins a silken shawl
against the grey squalls of advancing fall.
A laugh our wings are yet of willow,
a mercy our migration has turned this mellow
– by grace with you as gliding companion,
on these well-flown paths of gentle passion.

Keyhole
for my mother and father, now gone, still here

You know how light comes through a keyhole,
how it fans out into a dark room,
and how the dust motes drift
in that small delta of light?

And now you know
that this is an old story,
when keyholes were big
and shaped like chess pawns
or mushrooms, and your *child-self*
would lie awake, leaping inside
at the amber warmth
streaming in through that tiny belfry,
down the short hall from the living room,
where late into the night your mother and father,
aunts and uncles told rambling stories
around a worn wooden table
over perked coffee, peanuts and Mandarin oranges,
and how the clatter of voices would hush,
as though coasting to a stop on a gravel road,
at some scene of approaching clarity,
under parting clouds of denouement.

And how vast that pause.
Your breath in a bottle, your body an ear,
straining and hearing only the kitchen clock,
until a shell cracked,
a chair creaked, then another,
and some dam broke,
and shrieks of laughter swirled through the house,
sailed down from ceilings.

How sudden you rose
to the keyhole, but so afraid to look,
because you were sure
there was nothing out there
but God,
blazing away in laughter.
And of course,
it was.

For All That Is Given

I
Wind rushes past the reed and is transformed into sound.
The earth hums at the sign of light and calls up the evergreen.
Water rolls over rock and is given voice.

II
Moss thrives upon the fallen aspen.
Ants build beautiful cities in the trunk's heartland.
And what the aspen knew of the sun is given over to the ground.

III
The bow is drawn across the string.
The string quickens to sing within friction of horsehair and rosin,
filling in all the spaces between here and home.

IV
At the mouth of the cave sits the salamander.
Warm light spills in and the cool dark rock says *be still*.
There she balances between immense desires, perfectly moist.

Ode to Saskatchewan Towns Along the Yellowhead Highway

Let them say that he wrote crap poetry but loved the sound and feel of
words: terms, names, two, three or twenty at a time, coming together like
sprocket and chain;

like the names of prairie towns picketing by on the Yellowhead Highway,
rolling in his mouth: Langenburg, Churchbridge, Bredenbury;

bright words on green backgrounds, Saltcoats, Yorkton, Orcadia, Spingside –
sweet town of freshwater rising – rising south of Good Spirit Lake, where

he dreamed of a girl in the city of bridges, 200 hundred miles away, and he
had a black 1964 Chev Impala hardtop his friends called the Staff Car;

let them say he loved the long slow curve just east of Theodore where he
drove sensible and slow 'til he passed the Co-op service station and Motor
Hotel then cracked open the modest but decisive 2-barrel, 283 cu. in. V8;

and let them say, like they used to say, that he *hauled ass* all the way to the big
city – the evening coming on and the sun swinging low and the chrome trim
gleaming,

past Insinger, with Skynyrd singing *Freebird* around that banked bend by
the Holy Ghost Church, where he stood on the accelerator and the frame
creaked coming out of the curve – and the hood's silver molding sighted and
shot by Sheho,

tooled by Tuffnell, all four windows down in the airless heat with Foam Lake
floating on the horizon's treeless shimmer, below that green water tower you
can see for miles and miles;

rattling over the tracks, onward to Leslie, west by northwest with *Nantucket
Sleighride*, *Mississippi Queen* spitting dust up off the front speakers;

to Elfros, and the small bridge by the farm with five acres of car bodies;

waving at Mozart and coasting through Wynyard, past the bentgrass tufted
graveyard, and let them see how that big centre cross threw its shadow over
the Touchwood Hills;

on to Kandahar and down from the Steak House, the smell of cattle in the valley; sailing south of the saline shores of Big Quill Lake to Dafoe, where he'd come to a rolling

stop then steer north lifting that black body over Grand Funk tracks at 90 mph, then slow for the turn, west again; sweeping by the thousand hidden stories of Jansen, Lanigan, Guernsey;

let them say that by Plunkett, Viscount, Colonsay, the Impala was humming steady as time and cruising smooth and rhythmic as *Midnight Rider*, harmonious as *Suite: Judy Blue Eyes*;

into the cooling dusk of Elstow and Clavet, where, on the return trip, the Chevy's front-right retread flew off and went jackrabbiting into the ditch;

and let them recall that *Saskatoon* is a Cree word, beautiful and suitable for any old poet who quickens at the memory of high summer and grassland haze and a dark car with an 8-track

playing JJ Cale's *Call Me The Breeze* – those muffled beats and palm-damped chords pulsing and reaching right into his bones, *shuffling him on down Broadway with that green light, baby* …

We Need a Different Kind of Flesh

What we have is marvellous, but it lacks resilience.
I know this because once I was sitting in a café
                              sipping dark coffee,
and the light sifting through the windows
had this powdery softness
that sometimes comes early-to-mid-morning,
before surrendering to the brawny glare of afternoon.

And I had just noted this thought about light in my notebook,
when a silver-haired person wearing a lime neckerchief
                              and gardening shirt
rose to leave and, silhouetted in that full-flowering light,
signalled a simple acknowledgement of my presence.

And what rushed to fill me, inexplicable, irrepressible,
                              was joy;
so intense and primal that I would have been undone
                              had it endured.
Yet how I longed for it to endure
(which was unwise as I hadn't the frame for it).

It was this experience that compelled me to ponder an afterlife:
where at some forever-open café
                              we'll all be changed
and in a peach-tinted flash receive new flesh, new bones,
bodies made to bear ancient crimson flames,
                              and so,
go out into glad afternoons
                              magnificently naked.

Time of Salmon

First there is a thin black ribbon deep in the clear green water,
then a quick-rising cylinder of silver breaks the surface,
        a brief arch of twisting light, then,
as through a secret eyelet, a slipping under –
three quick flits of caudal fin and it's back
to a black outline leaving only a foamy embroidery of memory.

These green waters under the yellow spruce and red cedar,
stippled by coho making their last hard run upriver,
are older than the hemlock and fir,
older than the fissured face of the granite below.

This day is like the scale-flash of a breaching sockeye.
My best state is like a speck of spume here on the Capilano.
And together, *all my days are a handbreadth.*

From this wooden bridge I see my reflection,
variegated, fluid, drawn ribbon-thin downstream.

I am part river, my cells full of clear green water.
I am part Sitka and amabilis fir.
I am the pika and banana slug, the brown creeper, the chum,
I am the trail, burrow, branch, runnel, the run.

Should I decry the brevity of this life?
Does the salmon?

I am held

upon this earth by a stem: a picture of a yellow leaf sent by a friend; a quartz-rock collection glinting on a windowsill in a cinder-block basement; a field of tawny barley stooped and ready for cutting; a warm fall wind and the flashing white undersides of killdeer wings climbing higher, turning polished pewter;

a winding dirt trail with a green-grass mohawk and willow sides and the swale of Gypsy's back as she gallops for the barn, the bridle slack at her neck and me clutching her mane, her one thought of oats in the stall and my one thought to crouch low enough on that swayback to clear the header on the barn door.

There will be a day when my leaf falls. Until then I'll be here in the company of a chickadee – her mere-ness achingly like mine, her song, timeless.

It was a rare bird

but rare, to what measure? I wondered.
As rare as Blake's witness
of a faery funeral under a toadstool?

Oh, and now I envisioned heraldic greetings
at some international birding circle.

For it had a strange, elongated,
hammer-shaped head,
brilliant

as it flew with its brown-grey back and tail
shimmering with shades of red
from that wonderful head.

And I marveled:
was this my divine visitation,
my own luminous angel?

And I reasoned:
could the notion that language contains
ample signification
now be sustained?

Would all rhetoric reveal itself
at last, impoverished?

Was this the final proof
– if there was doubt –
of the reified continuum between sight and vision?

Or was this an instance of Hopkins' *inscape,*
delivered whole to my heart, by *instress,*
mystery made manifest?

What it turned out to be, in the end,
was a house sparrow with a rosehip in its beak,
beating a mad path toward a white pine.

Still, didn't it leave me with the idea
that one must love it all,
or die?

I Have Looked at Stars and Not Been Moved

At night, when I walk the short stone path down to the fire pit, I look up through the circle of poplars and listen.

At times the sky is sodden and mute, at times solemn and dark as pitch, darker still owing to the heavy shouldering of trees. Sometimes a pewter moon casts phosphoric light and I can hear with my inner ear a charcoal pencil zigzagging across the china-clay-paper ground, etching in the trunks, branches, shrubs, a birdhouse, the fine blades of grass to the hairs on the square stems of hemp nettle. And sometimes, like tonight, the sky is porous and profligate with stars.

Six thousand, give or take, are visible to the naked eye. One hundred thousand million in our own galaxy, on last count. Not one the same as the other. Millions of galaxies we know, and untold billions more we don't.

Stars look fixed, but they are fleeing and spreading at speeds hard to conceive. A trillion stars may look like one tight and friendly community. But distance deceives. Stars are lonely travellers, reclusive, remote, with little time for wandering minds.

Even the focused mind of Carl Sagan, a lifetime spent watching the shimmering, waiting for any new glimmering, could only touch the closest star – Proxima Centauri, just down the block at 4.2 light years – with the tip of his imagination.

O stars of wonder: laudable, luminous, with soft incandescent bodies. We see you in our dreams and on the foreheads of beautiful black horses; we throw you on flags to rally ourselves; we strive for your golden mark of celebrity.

O stars of wonder: giant spheres of hydrogen and helium, keeping unholy equilibrium between the grave compression of immeasurable gravity and the catastrophic force of thermonuclear blast, leaving oblations of energy for the use of eternity.

I have looked at stars and have not been moved. Perhaps there are greater sins. But tonight I'm an altar boy, an acolyte hurled as light through burning clusters of galaxies, blown to the ever expanding edge of the cosmos and back, never seeing the same splendour twice – red giants, white dwarfs – in the nova was the word.

And just as sudden, I stand, feet on flagstone, and the stars are drawn down around me as far as my ankles and are verified to be the warm bubbles of twinkling light I knew them to be as a boy, such that I put one in my pocket and return to bed.

Dear Friend
For Connie Howard (1956-2016)

Remember cycling down that steep road in *Kananaskis*
and I passed you? then you caught me and passed,
then me, you ('course these things never start
out as competitions), then the parking lot
came into view and you, crack-whip
timing, missile-focus, hurtled by,
your bike bobbing side to side
as you flew over the hard
earth, gravel and clay
disappearing
in the dust.
We laughed about it later
(you more than me)
bloody reckless, I think I said,
but what I wanted to say,
wish I'd had a way of showing you
what I carry with me (what,
for almost 30 years now?)
is that flash of smile
over your shoulder,
that flight of laughter, that
flaring arc of light in your eyes
as you passed me that last time.

The Lord's Prayer with Edits

Our God, who rides upon the heavens
and hides in every human heart,
give us this day a basement window
and a haze of thin branches
through which to view a waning moon.
Give us morning cut from the night like a bright cloth,
and a sun that runs like a calf through a field of flax in bloom.
Give us strength for daily pain and reasonable gloom,
but deliver us from the kingdoms of power and glory
and lead us to a round table in a walnut room
with wine from water and the mystery
of intimacy and everyday friendship.
Give us *this* day,
      it is bread enough.

BLUES

Almost Like the Blues – Ode to a Leonard Cohen Self-portrait

Eyes shaded by a forty-year-old fedora.
Lines of his face dark and deep as black poplar.
Stroke of mouth a grey branch or a row of whistling wrens.
Coat: light-sequined skeins of midnight mist, road dust and revelation.
Shirt collar frays from *contretemps* with a neck that resists every tie but one.
Shoes of bark and moss, soles are blue Cambrian clay.

He pauses for faces: frowns of doubt, creases of reticence,
sidelong casts of the disconsolate; and faces flowering with faith
that linger to marvel at a sky carved by scimitar wings of kestrels.
He loiters with the comic and deranged – all the outrageously unblessed.
He sits with gentle people, peaceful people, inquisitive folk who spend time
watching the *commedia dell'arte* of harlequins, Pacific loons and pelicans.

He greets the green witches who speak in wild mint and stinging nettle
and the two-spirited who teach the harmonies of many running waters.
He hails the sprites of pebbled creek beds that burble and blink
under the light of a sickle moon to signal the mystic flight of saints.
He foresees the god of thunder and just plunder who is coming
to batter our walls, rattle our orthodoxies, shatter our monopolies.

He likes blues: every smoke-smooth note bent deep into the next
and chords of mercy that go from minor to minor and still darker
and are resolved by not being resolved only negatively resolved in wonder,
not like our domestic wonder, but a wound, a gash in our data,
a blow to obeisance toward death, our techno-dogma of progress. These blues
he sings in coal-shaft basso, *almost like salvation, almost like the blues*.

Chicago

The skips come at night,
and only when conditions are right.
But when they come, mirroring their way
along a modulating ionosphere
for a thousand prairie miles, hitting
my copper wire, sliding down into the vacuum tubes,
I lie still as death,
supercharged, electric,
like an E-string ready to ring.

And through a crackling speaker I hear
Buddy Guy, Junior Wells, Muddy Waters
coming from WC-something in Chicago,
and suddenly I'm in a smoke-filled club deep in the soul
of Windy City and I'm the *Hoodoo Man,*
I'm the *Hoochie Coochie Man.*

Forty years later I'm sitting in *Jakes,* a Chicago pub,
corner of Superior and State,
and I tell my wife this story while Stevie Ray Vaughan's
Fender moods through overhead Bose speakers.

In a shiver I'm back in my blue plywood bedroom
lying on top of the covers at witching-hour,
copper wire buzzing, lighting up those tubes with six-strings,
mouth-harp flanging and popping at the speaker,
and I'm *Mannish Boy,* with arms wrapped around
Big Mama Thornton singing "Hound Dog,"
and the whole of summer
is coming in through that rickety window.

Small Town Prairie Café

Through these browning vinyl slats,
past the streaked pane,
in front of the corrugated metal wall of a tire shop,
is a shallow ditch and culvert
choked with calf-high quackgrass and dust-spackled dandelions.

A power pole is half in view, its anchor cable
with the dull-orange plastic protective tube,
pierces the hard-pan.
A mud-red half-ton is parked at the edge
of a cement lip that borders the ditch.

Inside, the harvest gold linoleum is cracked but clean,
my scalloped chrome diner stool complains to swivel,
the scoured Formica counter reflects
a buzzing fly-scat-peppered florescent tube
and under the bowed blades of an overhead fan

flows the grace of Gwendolyn,
who fills little porcelain pitchers with cream
and tops up the glass sugar jars,
brings me a heaping plate of fries,
gravy on the side and even more coffee,
spends her own quarter on the Rock-Ola in the corner,
and selects three songs: all
by The Lovin' Spoonful.

Making a Turn on View
for K. S.

Found perched on a concrete guardrail,
our Chevy Apache,
a discovery,
like we were coming at it with pickaxes,
a climb to a rich vein, with no stake to claim
except the bonanza to go on living.

It was raining, the highway was slick.
The Greyhound bus had crossed the line – it was said.
We swerved to miss, saw stone
cliffs and dark sky, cliffs and dark, dark on dark,
a drunken-dervish-whirl-around.

We slid backwards in a river of sparks,
front wheels, rear wheels gripping air,
a final solution of iron on rock,
until the hand of friction
forgave us our weight and impulsion.
On scale, not a pardon but a stay of execution.

On the rail the world rose silent.
Below the passenger door, small, flickering,
tucked in and asleep, Golden, B.C.

We huddled on the highway,
shoulders up against the dawn, keeping lit a shared cigarette.
K. said, *I coulda killed you all,*
and we waited – somehow relieved to see police.

But we did not tell them of the tank of gas, self-gifted
from the Shell on Shaganappi.
Or how the evening began without a plan,
in a slumping house by a hospital,
listening to *Grateful Dead's* "Anthem of the Sun."

We did not say how fevered memories paint
pacific suns over prairie beer joints,
or how kitchen table imagination does not equal experience
and deliver its flagrancy to the lap of lotus land.

Backs against the cinder-block shop, we waited
for the Chevy's verdict, while the rod and staff
of a morning sun stirred the glacial air,
and we slept.

Days later on Douglas, making a turn on View,
a tie-rod end dropped the terminal distance from shackle to asphalt,
leaving the truck to buck and lurch into the curb,
and something like scales fell from my eyes.
I laced up my shoes and hitched to the ferry.

The Prayer of a Man Called Moses Who Lives
Above the Cliffs at TransCanada's Mile Zero
a ghazal

Through a maze of oceanspray I watch clouds heap up over the strait.
Let your beauty be upon me Lord, if there is beauty.

Behind the broad grey column, the sun grows like a golden loaf.
May your joy feed me Lord, if there is joy.

I mend my net and fish, I shore up my shelter and sleep.
Let the work of my hands be anointed – for this is real work.

Masters throw sticks in the water; their dogs leap into the surf and paddle.
Early, my obedience was enforced, switch scars swim on my skin.

The wind rises, white tempests appear on the peaks of waves.
I knew crests of fear, troughs of absence – schooled amplitude of wrath.

In a gale, driftwood is driven against the granite.
I was hacked out of paternal bitterness – jagged mauls of malice.

A midnight road found my running feet and dawn came without difficulty.
If gladness abides, make me glad *according to the days* I've been afflicted.

But I was followed to these bluffs by thickets of conflict, thorns of torment.
Satisfy me now with your mercy, if mercy deferred can purge me.

Once I was full of promise, bright as your thought when the earth was formed.
Renew me by your power O God, if you are there … are you there?

Each day I bind up my rags, step out on this first mile, and wait.
Lead me Lord, if there is an exodus; if not, leave me an exit.

Inner-city Volunteer

This morning on my way to serve porridge,
            seeing you,
        I shunned you:

your shopping cart stagger,
that long wet shadow
                between your thighs,
those thin mucus trails
                across your face,
that odiferous ulcerous flesh.

I willed myself toward kindness
            and failed:
some sort of shared separating shame,
        I counselled myself.

Early that morning I read a verse of mercy and pledged,
            then
            let you walk by, unacknowledged.

You are not easy, you use ceramic cups as missiles,
you bruise your fists on walls,
you have, they say, mental health issues:
            far your fall
            deep your fear
            cold your hope.

When was the last time you laughed?
Not at someone's pain,
            but belly laughed,
            something truly funny.

When was the last time you were at peace?
Not by the needle's quick release,
            but by sitting
            astride the ocean,
            this ocean,
            mere blocks,
            I heard later,
from where you died.

Pine Needles

Pine needles fall in your hair
as you wheel the cart beneath the boughs
to stow the bottles and a blanket,
while the city escapes to a weekend.

Not Sheila, she will stay with you
into the glass-eye evening
of one more 40-ounce flush.

And in the dark, long past your old joke
about carbonated bear piss,
before the cold-forged morning,
when the shards of memory return

to rake the runnel of your back
and splinter the light in your eyes,
she will beg your indifference –
fearing the loneliness of your fists.

But she remembers, too, your tenderness
beneath the Tamarac, how you covered her
like a cotton blanket,
how you spoke together in the old way,
how her wisdom came to you like the dew.

And forgetting the hunger and the rage,
you both slept deep as dirt,
until the gardener woke you with his rake,
and you laughed past his glare and said, *Let
the fuckin' sprinklers come on, we need a wash.*

In those days Mistahi-muskwa's spirit
circled like the scent of snapped spruce,
and silence ran through the long grass
and the sky fell free of artificial light.

In the dream of those days
you held Sheila without trembling
as she curled like an *S* into your desire.
But tonight she is wary even of pine needles.

Reasonable Man

You're a reasonable man,
even in the heat
you've been
a paragon of calm.

You live in a neo-house
on a quiet cul-de-sac.

The satellite radio
in your Audi
plays *Sade*.

One day
inside
your little rolling bunker
on a bent road
you swerve
and blow your horn
long and loud
at a careless car
in U-turn,
the pressure
on the steering column
immense,
as though the harder you push,
the louder
your emptying roar,
until something passes
and you sit
bewildered
behind the windshield
and think:
no wonder there are wars.

Days of Grass

These are the days of withering grass,
of weeping thistle and wailing willow,
staggering lupines on pesticide paths
and brown winds blowing over plastic islands.

These are the days of hollow eyes walking
in hallowed towers with watching turrets,
of pink petunias on bullet-hole balconies,
of cryogenic kisses and libidinous missiles.

These are days of treaties torn
by shrivelled souls in vaunted chambers,
of brand-chocked brains and anal refrains
of mannequin minds in public office.

These are days of the corporate miser,
bailouts for the multinational, a
pittance for the children's hospital,
and poison for the neighbour's dog.

Now are the days of distant songbirds
of addled frogs beside strange waters,
of Arctic blues in long larval nights,
lost monarchs and the last burrowing owl.

These are the days of gorge and binge,
of hyper-cooled air for super-rich skin,
tracts of paved parking pleated by heat
and fabricated ponds under fold-away skies.

These are the days of metaphysical blight,
of electronic fugues and inner plagues,
genocidal hate and supremacist rage
down at the schoolyard shooting range.

These are the days of socialization
by pistol and penis and Phi Beta hazing,
recreational fury of the self-quarantined
and homicidal tyranny by touch screen.

These are the harried days
of the accelerated phrase,
and the acronymic end
to all discourse.

And where are the children of healing
who run for sweet-clover hills, and live,
still, for the music of whippoorwills,
in these dying days of grass?

Your Suicide

You told us once, *goodbyes*
held reason for acquaintances,
but friends cross all distances.
Now here we are, still casting shadows
under this fasting sun, and you
have sailed out on all your seasons.

We saw how spring's spear grass – barbs
tempered by summer's brittle heat,
riddled your path,
pierced your feet;

and how the late winter snows that blew
at night past your ice-white curtains
heaved you back into
frozen ruts.

What we didn't see was what you took to be
your final dream gutter out like a day moon,
divert you to a skeletal trestle
and send you tumbling in the wind.
But know this:
no final chaos can uncreate
your seven thousand sea-green suns,
your countless dawns in our collective hearts,
nor the streams of kindness in your eyes
that carried off the laws of time,
nor your light and laughter
that made us by our meetings richer.
Further on we'll know your absence
as the masquerade it is, once more
we'll see your smile on these shores,
your footprints outside our doors.
But here in your wake,
dear God, we ache.

Passing Through

Our bones are scattered at the grave's mouth,
as when one cutteth and cleaveth wood upon the earth (Psalm 141.7).

When the poplar is burl-free
you'll sight through it to the base
beneath, trace the axe's arcing edge
before lifting a hand, then succeed
its divide with a single swing.

When the spruce is cured but knotted,
your chosen piece a foot across and twice as deep,
when the axe, after a healthy overhand,
is buried by half and jammed, then,
clean-and-jerk axe-and-block,
and when the fettered affair
reaches that weightless crest above
your head, let it turn, about-face;
and with inveterate eye, guide
its fall toward the chop-block,
causing the axe head's
blunt back to strike first.

And the spruce length's weight,
tripled upon the skyward wedge,
will part its wooden body.
A satisfaction,

even though you know
each temporal arch
that cleaves the air
crops the creep of sun,
splits the night,
rends your hopes –
hews flesh from frame,
hip from socket, tooth from jaw,
'til your bones
scatter on the ground,
pass through the earth
and out of every mind.

Mercy Is an Old Word

This morning at Credo, a homeless person suffering the mental and physical strafing of street life, stole in and began to panhandle, and just as quickly was ushered out. We lowered our heads in that half-guilt, half-relief pose of the considerate-privileged, and returned to our coffees.

This afternoon in Beaver Hills Park, a girl with a brick is threatening another girl. She holds the brick high over her head with both hands, screaming, *you fucking-whore-crack-fuck-bitch, I'm going to kill you.*

Three males and an older girl are watching, standing around them, taking turns trying to calm her, saying, *calm down you stupid cunt, fucking nutcase, bitch, you cow.* This goes on for too long and my insides are vibrating and I'm getting ready to call 911. But she gives in and runs off, throwing the brick in the bushes.

Now a man comes yelling, shrieking in bursts, howling much of the same vitriol into the air – at no one anyone can see. Another man is collecting cigarette butts he finds by benches. He lifts each one to his nose, his mode of selection.

There's a tree in this inner-city park I've photographed over the years. Last year it still leaned supernally over the ornamental pond. This year it has been cut down and the pond left dry.

Mercy is an old word, it's a love word, a glory word, a release word, but over the years its religious, not-of-this-world overtones have parched it, stripped its green, rotted its core, chopped it down to a stump.

Caged

Under the noonday fulgent glow of a pine-sifted fall sun,
high above the scooped walls and dark-eyed potholes of the Sooke River,
over the rainstick swish of my bike tires on fine grey gravel, I hear
the faltering flute solo of a low stream crossing a stone embouchure.

On the schist crust of tilting bedrock are thinning mats of moss
and the loose scurf of silver lichen;
in the scoured canyon loosely moored to a sweating ledge
a line of wildflowers lift their faces to the jute light.

Rolling by a lone wren perched on a branch of wrinkled berries,
past the departing glances of a hundred unseen eyes,
I come to the barb-strung top of an elevated wire fence
that shields the fresh water catchment area for the city of Victoria.

And the red sign riveted to the locked steel gate reads:
We are sorry. But what gives life must now be caged
or it too will flee up the folds and flanks to the peaks
and into the mist-less blue jewel sky.

If I Were To Do It All Over Again

Let me say this up front,
        (so as not to bore you with a tidy circular ending to this poem,)
that if I were to do it all over again,
there's much I would do just the same.
That said, if I could do it all over again,
I'd seek wisdom earlier,
the honeyed wisdom of the free:
who are not run by the approbative nod,
who do not collect bits of junk identity,
who live as though death has passed.
If I were to do all over again,
I would not pull down the nests of wasps.
I would not have sought to make a porcupine my pet,
nor strove to teach a crow to use my shoulder as a perch.
I would give myself to lilacs at every opportunity.
I would be obedient to the rhythm of rivers.
I would allow meaning to grow in its own garden,
and not rip it up and place it on a metal table for dissection.
I'd do the same with faith.
I would learn to look at myself kindly, with love, and if not love
at least forgiveness, which is a form.
I would grow more tomatoes and hill my potatoes before they flowered.
I'd learn the language of trees, sit under the tutelage of elm or elder
and every morning rediscover
that I'm a guest here,
here under the sweep of limbs and white clouds,
always just a guest,
a worker ant, a fuzzy colourful worm, a bee in a vineyard,
as are we all.
I would pray more and accept the contradictions of prayer.
Every day, I'd climb into my attic to challenge God,
and every day, by grace, I'd be thrown further out,
into a deepening lake of bright complexities.
I would tolerate less to make room for more love.
I would be a disciple of gratitude, an acolyte of contentment.
I would read less Dostoyevsky and more Dr. Seuss.
I would hang a sign in my kitchen that says:
Do not look for a sign, carry on without one.
I'd find a way into my own form of activism and not fear being disliked.
I'd welcome paradox and confusion but be impatient with stupidity,
especially my own.

I'd spare myself the suffering and grief of comparison.
And even though Georgina was a grade ahead of me
I would have risked telling her I liked her:
those days when *like* meant being half-tipsy in her presence,
enveloped in wonder at the sight of her yellow blouse,
her white-blond hair,
shining,
even in the shadows.

Blues – A Self-portrait in Twelve Bars

I am the alpha blue of dark stars
I move over canopies of cottonwood
brood down brindled boughs

leak through lengthening catkins
to fall into the grey cones of your eyes
I'm the elysian wish that runs

through cerulean hills of your childhood
and the blue burst of spider veins
spreading over the aging cheek of desire

I'm rain caught in the cleft of your heart
a columbine cluster of tears at your canthus
I'm the blue-spark-stream of acetylene torch

piercing the steel cast of your secret cares
and cobalt coat of cooling dreams
I'm the sapphire flicker of water strider

on a spring slough in summerfallow
I'm a bustle skirt burlesque of blue flames
shimmying in late fall's deadfall bonfire

I'm a blue tattoo of bracket fungus on birches
where jays wheedle, chirr and chuck
in the lavender luminance of dusk

I'm the translucent edge of arctic ice
under the sun's avenging creep
I'm Delta Blues' muddy runnel murmur

that runs 'til June – the bluest of months
I'm the moon's powder blue resplendence
falling on some stone-headed sage

I'm the *bleu céleste* of your love's robe
and cracked enamel
of their cup and kettle

I'm the indigo ache of too much beauty
too much sorrow
the dew-droop of mourning

and the midnight blue *cortège* of ravens
riding the dawn winds
of earth's omega

HOLY GOATS

Holy Goats

Weighty flakes of wet snow are falling at five in the morning. They drop like damp rags past the saffron globe of street light. Appreciate them for their lack of presumption. They have nowhere else to go, aren't looking to make anything more of themselves. Unambitious? Yes, you could say that. But say it without derision.

Consider the zeal of their capricornian indifference. Goats, after all, are just as much part of this world as lemurs. Which would make an appropriate theme for a paper expounding upon our pluralistic planet.

Your professor would explain the hidden homogeneity of things within the intoxicating singular thingness of the universe. She would do this, of course, without detracting a micron of individuality from any microcosm, thereby further burnishing the unseen sheen of the entire cosmos. And at the candle of night in her leather chair with her glass of Aberfeldy and her cat draped over an arm she would weep into the fullness of life lived with such knowledge.

Across the city an ordinary man, glimmered at by a shred of reflected yellow light coming in past the silhouette of a snow-thickened branch, unaccountably sees himself through the distant eyelet of that slim light, and suddenly understands: gift of place, blessing of belonging, the holiness of his own goatishness.

Now the snow is thinning, as it does when the temperature-droop of dawn arrives and the stars drive blind behind clouds. The bursting ordinary clouds. The bountiful raggedy snow.

My Sister Elizabeth Teaches Me To Ride a Bicycle

Always, there was Mrs. Spilchen's caraganas,
ready to hang my forays up for ridicule.
And across the street, Mrs. Kreiger's clay petunia pots,
unnerving for the penalty they implied –
greater, I feared, than these first scrapes
on my face and forearms.

Once more I hear coaxing mixed with caution.
My sister stands firm,
grips the seat to steady the red frame.

Once more I climb and straddle the Schwinn.
Now the push,
the slight downhill grade,
the front tire tremble,
the lurch and looming pitch,
then poise to counterpoise,
and past my grandmother's house I gain balancing-speed.

And just here, if I had had the time,
I would have shown you the science
that proved this boy and balloon-tired bike
the centre of the universe.

But I have other things on my mind: the wind
shocking my hair, whip-willow body
bending into the hill past the Baptist church,
riding up the horizon of White Rose Gas,
Springside Café, Skea's General Store,
dirt alleys angling away in my wake,
all the way up Main, to Railway –
with no thought of the coaster brake.

Steering a circle at the Credit Union
begins the mortised procession of pool hall,
barber shop, dry goods store, post office, hotel, lumber yard,
on up past the Esso, where I turn west,
cross the train tracks,
sight Elysium.

Now I hear car tires and veer sharp into sow thistle,
fall under the frame, embed gravel in elbows,
and know my sister's absence.
Nothing to do but stand on one pedal,
hop half a block on one foot,
swing my leg up and over,
graze crotch on crossbar,
recall small flesh flags on caragana branches,
push down, feel the chain tighten, reach equilibrium, and
let the world once more roll beneath me like a log in water.

Roll past the brick school, the yellow bus, the big city,
the birthdays, anniversaries, children.
Past cenotaph, town hall, its bell tolling out
the losses that signal the end of this balancing act.
The slackening chain, missing teeth, bent spokes, broken links,
loss of wind, the downhill drift,
the preference for little else.

West of town there's a dismount where
I'll leave my bike to the rust-seeking rain,
released to lean on its kickstand,
as a book on a shelf
I'll not open again.

The Saturday morning in May

was fresh and bright
and our house was still, no
patter, no muted breakfast banter,
no creak in the floor, father
was not leaning back in his chair shuffling papers,
sister made no rustle, mother, no kitchen clatter.

Coming downstairs,
pausing on the landing I knew:
The Rapture had happened.
The front door was flung open,
as were (I was sure) all the doors
of other Baptist households in the village, and I
   was *left behind*,
and the spring day sunk bleak and brooding.

I ran outside in a blur, turned
toward the street. *Silence.*
I raced to the back of the house,
   where my mother was hanging up laundry.

The day returned in a blaze,
twice fresh, twice bright,
my mother a vision,
a radiant angel,
beautiful as she stretched and stood on her toes
   defiantly pinning white sheets to the sky.

Sometimes while driving a dirt road beside a blooming canola field

all things become simple, exquisite, undivided.
Yellows flow unframed and unforced through greens and blues.
The road rises up its wedded hill, trees bow to the east,
and grass makes a serenade of the wind's silence.
Then there are memories, and then complexity.

Sometimes from my chair in the cabin,
through the mullioned triangle of window near the peak,
just above the swaying seaweed of poplar tops,
I see a sunrise reflecting pink on the hulls of clouds,
and think, Oh, to stay in this warm dark submersible,
sail mystery's slipstream and never surface.
Then the sun rises higher and the pink-hulled ships slowly sink.

Sometimes in a dream, Christ comes to share a beer and talk;
we talk of sparrows, vineyards, the smell of fresh sawdust,
the taste of fish fried over a coal fire.
Then things get awkward, as we have little else in common –
except (while dissimilar) a knowledge of sorrow.

So before I go I tell him I'm grateful for the green arts
of those who parse plants for the healing within.
Grateful for bread, wine, salt and song; grateful
for the dogged love that still broods over our mournful lives.
For these, I say, I will be your scribe
and write my letters large for as long as I last.
And just then I feel a stuck door in me move.

But for an otter

he calls Amos,
a thousand driftwood orphans,
some reasonably good throwing rocks
and a cigar for rumination,
he sits alone on an ancient bleached log
blowing Nicaraguan smoke over the Juan de Fuca Strait,
sifting his many cares.

I know, he says, looking over at Amos,
I'd have made a ridiculous Buddhist,
attached as I am to suffering the shrinking gates of tomorrow,
fretting some feverish future.
As it is, he adds, *I fail the bar of half-assed Christian.*

Sitting in that fragrant acrid cloud
by the swaying skirts of eelgrass and choirs of kelp and shell
he waits for some solicitous sand crab to move his beached heart
into a tidal font of hope.
And looking across the strait he watches
the lilac light play on a far wave and hears Amos say,
Worry is prayer, old friend.

Daily Office – James Bay Waterfront

This short commute to my daily office,
like winning some holy lottery: held

to lose my *self* to the grand humility of rock and lichen,
kelp beds, eelgrass meadows and tide pools,

to watch the narrowing sea between granite shoulders
blinking with starfish, ringing with jellyfish,

chalky with chitons, spiny with urchins,
and shore crabs scuttling silently on the floor of a rock pool,

to sit, until my eyes bring down comet tails
and the stars break into spindrift,

to be reconciled to my rightful pool
on God's botanical beach, and

leaving my burdens to the Scotch broom bluffs,
I steep in slow galactic joy …

Is this to know
something of the ultimate?

And why – among the congregations of gooseneck
barnacles and rolling blooms of sea anemone –

strive for anything less, or more,
than the company of a cobbled beach?

Yet for all this intimate *hereness*, I return
(or I'm returned), to the veiled world

of time and happenstance, hoist bike and bag
and shuffle on down the shore –

one more disordered aspirant
for the Order of Holy Fools.

Last Night's Storm

Eight windows in this room, nine with the skylight.
So, when you are lying in bed and a storm moves at midnight,
and lightning rides through the trees, rinsing leaves white,
you may think of the apocalypse, or you may think
you are drinking at the shining river of God's pleasure.

And when the spiderwebs on the ceiling flash,
fat with light, and walls blaze magnesium bright,
you may see Thor and hear the rage of a hundred weathered gods.
Or see a fountain of light that showers bodies with love.

And at that illumination you may be struck dead with regret
for every failed encounter and opportunity ignored,
for each nursed resentment and bitter epithet.

Or, you may be pulled above the covers by silken strings,
lifted by a sudden flood of forgiveness to sail the weave
of a silver web and emerge at the delta of all creation,
where history is reconciled and time redeemed.

And when the storm passes and all your thoughts
collapse like thunder upon this weighted world,
you may be wiser for the courtship of excess
but happy to return to the quotidian fold.

Hard Red Spring

The day I stood on the clipped grass of Olds College –
after palming Norquay, Chinook, and Neepawa
until my fingers had unlocked their doors
and I could smell the loam and feel the wind
and see three months of rain and heat
in an amber seed of Hard Red Spring wheat
– I saw kaleidoscopic rings around the sun.
And at the sun-dog ends of those high-noon rims
were more rings intersecting, and at each intersection,
like Ezekiel's wheels in wheels and ever-moving eyes,
were more rings, until the sky was bejewelled
like the pierced lobes of a thousand harlots.
And I had just read *The Late Great Planet Earth*,
and my girlfriend told me she was pregnant,
and I bought a *Living Bible* and raced back to my room,
to wait for the rapture, the tribulation, the millennial reign,
that wouldn't come by naming, only by fasting,
that would keep safe the obsequious
but confound the concupiscent,
and condemn all the students
of Human Development.

And I waited.
And the morning came and my girlfriend arrived on the bus.
We moved into the basement of a pagan.
And I again bought cigarettes and blew circles of smoke
in the back yard, behind a hedge, hidden from the horizon,
to try and keep her safe from my own piebald imaginings.
But I was chained by eschatology
and feared being only *almost ready*.
And it was a long zionic hangover before the haze would lift.
A long time sifting chaff and spotting blight and blotch,
so as to see kernels as kernels and crops without circles.
Until, releasing my recommitted virginity,
I could grow a sprout at the germ-end of self-mercy,
and glimpse again an epiphany in a grain of wheat
without needing to be stunned above the eye by a harvest moon,
hurled by Mary Grace across some doctor's waiting room.

Covered in Yellow Light

When you're walking Ogden Point breakwater at sundown, covered in yellow light, watching the silhouette of the Olympic Mountains sharpen under a near-full moon that's climbing above the Clover Point cliffs, holding hands with Deb, her palm cool on yours, and you pass a young couple fishing, a small lamp beaming between them as they cast their lines into a sea so still that the rigged spoons ring out as they clap the water, and when a small dog bounces on the concrete walkway as she watches a great blue heron full of patience, standing on an island of bull kelp studying a place just beneath the surface of the ink-green ocean, and when you approach the lighthouse at the end of the breakwater and see its orange flashes soaked up by the dusk, while a pilot boat pliés past toward a container ship to help steer it through the Strait of Juan de Fuca, and a girl with dyed deep-red hair glows down on the rocks, courting only quietude while watching the far shore transform under a bruised peach sky, and at her back the moon runs its nickel ribbon along the salt water kissing every ripple on its way to meet the rising water in your own eyes: you'd be persuaded to believe that all the world has ceased its strife.

Lead Boots Blue Sky

For a sky this blue you need lead boots to keep from flying up.
I learned the hard way: One morning I stepped outside,
looked heavenward, noted the sheer depth of blue and began to rise.
I reached for the ladder of the spruce tree by our front step
but wasn't equal to the magnitude of lift and it slipped through my fingers.
I gathered speed. Our house shrank.
The city became a cerulean map with microdots moving along fading lines.
The air was a vast sea that sought to push me to its surface.
An indigo intensity deepened as the oceans came into view.
The curve of the earth tightened and I was lost in azure.
I shut my eyes, focused on the fawn-browns of fall –
still, clamorous trains of blue steamed through my mind.
Approaching the poison shores of ether I breathed, released,
mused on shades of earth while rapidly repeating a string of mantras
that came, as it were, out of the blue – *soil, summer-fallow,*
clay, loam, dust, humus – and flew straight down
with such speed I'd have shattered the sidewalk.
But I invoked the gods of green, came mindful
of verdant grass swaying in mesic rangeland;
I channelled canola fields in bright citrine bloom
and floated down slow as a winged seed,
landing on our front step.

Deb was just coming out of the bathroom and asked
if I would make scrambled eggs for breakfast.
I said I was happy to but needed to go shopping later.
At the scuba diving store I asked if they carried any lead boots.
The sales lady said, *We only have one pair left.*
I'd like to buy them, I said.
You're the seventh person this week to buy lead boots!
What's going on?
I don't know, I said, *but I'll need them when my meditation is off.*
God, she said, *I love this town.*

Arnold Christopherson – Custom Harvester, Beat Poet Welder

Arnold, who likes his last name but wishes
it started with a K, like Kris's,
stands outside his machine shop,
steel-toe Kodiaks planted hip-wide and sole-deep
in cinder, slag and oil slick,
on his head a welder's cap
and helmet cocked up like a satellite dish.

Behind him, big bay-doors thrown open to April.
At the threshold a steel beam rests on pitted concrete,
has a perfect stringer-bead, glowing kidney-red.

He's building trailers for Cockshutt combines
that will take us south to the red spring, durum
and winter wheat of America's midwest.

Squinting away the grey curl from an Export A,
Arnie inhales the main drag of Springside, and confides
that the blue arch of a 7018 rod is thought,
that alloy is voice, that metal is diction,
and welding is conviction.

Steps back, clicks on buzz box, snaps in fast-freeze 'lectrode,
flips down face shield and grooves a down-hand weld –
spark belch, white-hot tip, precise plying
and slow pressure of tensile tongue,
sudden parting of bright steel lips
and slow weave away, like the cool trace of a finger
across a closed mouth.

*

It's summer, and we've crossed the border,
and Arnie has switched polarities.
Stop at a blondish bar outside Bismarck.
Rounds of Michelob and Arnie's taking bets.
I join the line, crumple my wrist on his midriff,
move on, don't grimace.
Next morning, greasing machines, he grins at me.

Deeper south now, daily wheel of daybreak cafés,
Tammy Wynette with bacon and eggs,
thousand-mile windrows,
rain scat and rattlesnakes,
salt pills for heat,
afternoons that grow ancient,
and grain-dust sunsets that sear the nights.
The work ends, boy, when the straw goes tough.

Going home, his Silverado hides in the slant
of a South Dakota sun,
and I back a loaded grain truck into the driver's door.
We settle at the end of September.
Left me enough for a Yamaki 12-string.

Home, midnight, Halloween, with friends,
we roll his trailers out on Main,
barricade the bay-doors with rusting bones
of farm machines, buried out back
under Canada thistle and couch grass.

Late afternoon next May, outside the shop after rain,
Arnie says *You're on the crew if you want it.*
I say, *I'm not doing much else.* He nods,
peels back crisp silver foil, lifts out a cigarette,
offers me one, steps back, lights up with a benzene torch,
inhales, lowers the glowing cherry from his lips,
gazes up over the CN tracks, says, *Forgot*
to thank you for rescuing all that iron.
Salvaged some I-beams for framing,
some angle-iron, for bracing.

And I, following his gaze, see the fall yield ferrous fields,
see I-beam rhizomes, spring-steel tillers,
wrought-iron sheath, ligule and leaf.
I see a million lucid kernels receive the light
of meaning at the silver confluence of sowing and reaping.
And squinting away the blue of a small prairie town,
Arnie and I exhale, wait upon the ripening
to take us down, one more time, into that glory.

If I had a name like Wendy Morton
for Wendy Morton, after her poem "If I had a name like Rosie Fernandez"

I would wear braids of bluebells,
and a shawl of wild indigo.

I would sleuth the understorey of old-growth forests,
packing pistils of Peruvian lilies,
finding clues under cloak ferns.

I would transcribe the weave of wind in willows.
I would publish the loop and sweep of cliff swallows.

If I had a name like Wendy Morton
I would serve lavender tea to every stranger
willing to waltz me
through a pink blizzard of blossoms.

I'd buy a purple satchel
and stalk the autumn equinox
to forage a pot of filigreed collards.

I would walk on water
wearing pontoon shoes
of pumpkin shells.

I would lounge with sea lions
– we'd watch the geysers of orcas.

I would sit with a young Inuit poet
– we'd find the shortest path to each other's heart.

I would take all the turbulent minds,
the hijacked dreams,
our fears of flying,
and lyric them into oblivion.

Oh, if I had a name like Wendy Morton,
I would shush the mortal creak and moan
and bring on everlasting spring
with a single poem.

The Tree Northeast of the Legislature Buildings in Victoria, B.C. Circa 1974

We had a good thing going,
living under that 70-foot Sequoia,
the way those graceful branches reached
around and down to the ground, creating
a natural domicile.

Daily order of business:
    morning constitution in the oak-trimmed east-wing washroom;
    bicameral stroll on Wharf and Government Street;
    standing committee on the location of affordable clam chowder;
    caucus meeting in the shade of the Empress Hotel,
    at consideration: the beauty of masonry covered in Boston ivy;
    afternoon sitting: on the walls of Inner Harbour,
    legislating among the long-legged, tube-top tourists;
    sunset assembly at the Beaver Pub, royal prerogative:
    terry-towel tablecloths and twenty-five cent draft,
    debates, rebuttals, proposals, and 2 AM adjournment –
    full slate of meetings, appointments, consultations – important work.

We were in session every day that summer.
It was all going well, until the day someone was moved,
private members' bill notwithstanding,
to hang his laundry on the outside of the tree.
The Sergeant-at-Arms could not feign inattention,
not in the middle of the august Packard Convention,
not with all those tweed-capped, leather-elbowed tax-payers,
and their calabash whalebone pipes,
broguing about their sixteen-cylinder road boats.
The dissolution of parliament was immediate.

It was a miserable winter on Salt Spring,
in those plastic tents that did not prorogue
the damp and the cold.
And the sound of unremitting rain on the fly-sheet
was not romantic.

Baptism

I'm splayed out under the Chrysler,
beneath an oil-plumed shroud of power train
– drive shaft, U-joint, differential puzzle –
bolting a rear axle leaf-spring to the frame,
every crease of me greased black,
right knuckles bloody, red
from the lug-nut screw-up of a left-hand thread.

I'm jack-ready to kick out the blocks,
but the brakes still need bleeding,
and I'm a body, one bridge
and ten miles short
of a carousal of cousins,
all born with quivers full of wrenches
in the middle of an explosion
of mismatched car parts,
the strewn luxury of searchable wreckage,
that waits for the next nut-popping grunt
and *goddam-rust* and wrenched-free cheer.

In my mind I'm already rolling up in the Windsor,
shirtless bodies descending from haystacks,
and rounds of backwoods-Bohemian back-slaps.

And that's how I come to pray,
long past late, without impunity,
at the crest of the river hill
inside three tons of brakeless menace,
wheels spitting gravel,
two fat twisters tailing back tires,
and the grille flying hard at the Whitesand River
running two feet above the single-track bridge.

Even a fool finally finds gravity,
for in the sudden sunless entombment
and the brackish baptism of a spring flood
I feel the truth of every road.
Dark, ramified, refracted.

And in that moment, protracted,
I am truth reified,
born of water and spirit,
born beneath a bend of road,
born under a sign
that on this side of the bridge
we drive blind
under a dreamt-up sun
guided by some rumoured map
of received memory.

I wheel east, then north,
as over the windshield
the waters divide
and the blue fenders rise
and the spring returns,
bathed and blazed by light,
so full, as if the sun itself
had been riven by joy,
ridden by love.

A woman on *The Queen of Oak Bay*

is twisting a tress of white hair
around her right index finger.
In her left hand is a phone, into which she speaks
verdict and sentence against men.

She arraigns a dark reunion:
They will be riding the ferry to the mainland.
They will gather at the stern,
where she has arranged beer and chips for Cliff,
tea with three spoons of sugar for Jerome,
and Pinot Gris in a stemless glass for Lance.

And while the men drink and gawk and await
the reason for their summoning, she will pluck
each deplorable one of them off the deck,
as one would a stray hair on a sleeve,
and drop them into the Georgia Strait,
burying them at sea,
as it were.

Her friends will emerge and there will be drinks on the sun deck,
and the happy jangled notes of harpsichord and flute
(how Cliff hated flute)
will skip over the grey-green breakers, their crests
white and frothy as freshly popped champagne
(Jerome thought champagne sour).
There will be clinking of glasses and *sons-a-bitches!* cheers,
and of course, there will be dancing
(yes, Lance was too pretentious to dance).

The captain on the bridge, a sensitive soul, will turn the ferry south,
then west through the Strait of Juan de Fuca, out to the high seas,
to sail in large graceful trans-boundary circles.

Oh there will be much carrying on,
there will be laughter, love and release,
regardless of the mist.

(She could have endured the mist, was prepared for storms,
and to live without flute and dance, yes, even that.
But not with arms that once vowed warmth yet drove away her worth.
Not with tides of fear that forbade her show a trace of tears.
Not exiled from friends that kept her light aloft.)

After the party everyone on board will forget
what must be forgotten,
and the ferry will turn back to the mainland.

The men beneath the Pacific will have, by now,
come out of their flesh
and entered the bodies of sea urchins.
(A creature, say marine biologists,
that has the capacity for remorse,
without means for its expression.)

Ashamed of their small imaginations,
they will renounce their spiny tyranny.
And as they sit on the floor of the ocean,
they'll be given the notion
that salvation and resurfacing
will come with explicit contrition,
or when the sea goes perfectly still.

The white-haired woman will put down her phone,
watch the valanced waves drape Bowen Island,
watch the mist lift above the spindrift
and smile at the sea
that has never been still.

People Retire All the Time – Today Is My Time.

I've been asked what it feels like:
I say, it's like a blind curve on a dirt road,
and you're in the red 1965 Pontiac Parisienne,
and you just got your licence
so obviously you want to test
the 327 cubic-inch engine,
with its double-barrel carburetor,
because you only have the car for the weekend.

Or, perhaps, I'll confide, it's like finding
you're finally free to talk about those
Epicurean quirks you hold dear,
that have no location within the reign of reason,
yet seem sensible within themselves
– things like, knowing you sing better
when wearing burgundy underwear,
and accepting that retirement
is simply the state of affairs
where it gets harder and harder
to find burgundy underwear.

Or it's like walking in a wind
on the crest of a prairie hill,
where the swirling leaf,
the snapping flags
of torn birch bark
and bent grass
have pooled
their angular
momentum,
dissolving the lines,
melting all into motion
except here and there where
your eye comes to rest, arrests,
and frames again the forms of leaf,
bark, grass, for one more resurrection.

Or, like today, it's revisiting a calling,
returning to that park full of memory,
full of inner-city beauty and squalor,
to recline at the root of things,
to drill down through the core of yourself
to the dark night of your identity,
to the grass-mat packed-dirt
lowliness of each of us,
each within our own glorious
brand of selfishness

holding up our one tremulous light
high enough to see elm, gull, elder,
bench, beggar, bottle, you, me, us,
brilliant with being,
magnificent with offering –
and you run through the streets
carrying this news to the end.

Writing in the Dark

Writing in the dwindling dark under a short eve,
    rain in recession, sky's roof rolled into view,
I can almost believe words have sway
    to lift me whole and alive into reality.

Like this rain-wrung sky flowered into view,
    I am becoming what once I could only name,
resolved whole and harmonic into the deep real.
    Dissolved is the wall between thing and name,

I am become what I proclaim:
    dark, light, eve, roof, sky, rain;
fallen the wall between symbols and *their-selves*,
    my *self* a vessel for things in *themselves*,

dark, light, eve, roof, sky, rain,
    boy inside buoyed to re-embark,
my *self* a vessel yet blessed as *self*,
    under this short eve in the dwindling dark.

Saved

Blossoms bleed in the churn of ocean winds.
Hearts die for want of flight.
Visions evaporate.
These are things you understand.

But one dawn a bird flew past your window
and by that simple act your heart opened like a flower.

Was it the faint summer-pink against the birth of blue?
Was it the distance?

Far enough that the bird took a long moment to pass?
Far enough to say that it was every bird in one bird?

Was it the wings of light flashing in the void?
Was it some cardinal link furnished by separation?

Because in the open palm of arrested time
you felt, between you, a fine-spun thread.
Not slack or you would have missed it.
Not tight or it might have snapped.

What was it?
A transcontextual connection?
A deep unknowing?
Love?

This thing that left you lounging in the throat of a lily
on the porch of eternity.

That was far away and long ago.
Yet you still use the timber of that memory
to shore up your misshapen life.

In Praise of Things You've Seen

I
Two friends hug in greeting
then talk while holding each other by the elbows.
Even from across the street their profiles bear a kind of light,
like creation.

II
Years after your dad passes away you see his smile
on the face of a man taking short careful steps across a parking lot,
so recognizable that your heart does a little leap.
You always loved seeing his smile from that angle,
the way his mouth shaped an open surprise,
the way his eyes came bright under his brow and how
the creases at his eyes gathered and deepened
like ripples on a northern lake.

III
You're with your son having a beer in an outdoor patio,
he sits there like a swagger draped over a chair
then suddenly runs half a block to retrieve a fallen grocery receipt
for a man with a walker. And you know
he would have run halfway across the city.

IV
There's a young woman at a small round table in a coffee shop.
Around her neck is a sheer scarf, one fallen end is draped
over a stack of books and spills over the edge of the table.
The forefinger of her left hand winds a loose lock of auburn hair.
Her right hand lightly touches her neck
while her elbows rest on the oak-top table, almost weightless.
The extraordinary warmth of ordinary light
falls through a window over her shoulders to the floor
while her grey eyes reach across to her partner
in the secret conversation everyone knows:
in praise of every little thing.

Beatitudes Without Attitude

Blessed are the unassuming:
    for theirs is the kingdom of gratitude.
Blessed are the rivers:
    for they shall carry away the burning boats of sorrow.

Blessed are the apostates of money and power:
    for theirs is the domain of freedom.
Blessed are the still waters:
    beside which we shall be led.

Blessed are those who ignore the fascination of the herd:
    for they shall escape hook, line and sinker.
Blessed are the prairie sloughs:
    where beds of cattails host red-winged romances.

Blessed are those who topple the idols of mass culture:
    for they shall be called curators of light.
Blessed are the Great Grey Owls:
    given to the charity of twilight.

Blessed are the eyes of sculptors and painters:
    for theirs is the realm of sight.
Blessed are the spiralling, hovering gulls:
    given for the pleasure of wind.

Blessed are the hands of potters:
    for they shall be called stewards of the second chance.
Blessed are the flitting wrens that flurry ornamentals:
    for theirs is the provenance of happiness.

Blessed are the hands of hospice workers:
    for theirs is the coming reign of mercy.
Blessed is the waggle dance of bees:
    world of intelligence, truth and understanding.

Blessed is the rising sun, the enduring earth, the forgiving seas:
    hear their groans of longsuffering grace.
Blessed is the risen heretic:
    whose here, now and how is love.

Ordinariness

I live on the ordinary margins.
And not in any marginal way, no,
in quite an ordinary way.
I sit down easily in an ordinary day,
feel the ordinariness down to my common bones.

I do not desire obscurity or anonymity.
I'm like you, a bit of attention is nice.
But I could never claim a cutting edge.
That ledge is so crowded these days,
and everybody else is thinking outside the box.

No, I'm quite leafless in the winter,
and a common shade of green in summer.
And I'm not fond of a long Latin phrase thrown in,
or speech with arcane allusions to abstruse myths
that parts me from the soil, regular suffering
or the weaned-child-quiet of my soul.

Of course the request of my attendance
to the gowned procession will not come.
So is it any wonder that I can't stop looking at you?
In you I desire nothing but my effacement.
Nothing but to blend into your unbroken bones.

Acknowledgements

"Poem Broken Open" and "Last Night's Storm" first appeared in *Earthshine Magazine.*

"Grain Elevator Scene Circa 1979" and "Ode to Saskatchewan Towns Along the Yellowhead Highway" were published in *Prairie Fire* (Winter, 2018).

"Hard Red Spring," "Baptism" and "Chicago" first appeared in *There Are No Small Moments* (The Rasp and The Wine).

"Pine Needles" was published in the small anthology, *Gettin' Gritty Inner City,* where, curiously, for winning 3rd prize it was also translated into Japanese.

An earlier version of "Blue Sky Lead Boots" was published in *Emerge 17* (Simon Fraser University).

An earlier version of "Beatitudes Without Attitude" was published by *Christian Courier.*

Thank you to the poetry community gathered in various venues in Edmonton, Alberta, where a number of these poems were first tried out. And to Planet Earth Poetry in Victoria, B.C., thank you for welcoming me with warmth and letting me try on some of my newer west coast poems (and some prairie ones).

Thank you to the intimate and vital SFU Writer's Studio poetry cohort of Emily Olsen, Viola Prinz, Cara Waterfall and our poetry and lyric prose mentor, Fiona Tinwei Lam, for helping me weed and water a number of these poems. More, thank you for cheering and celebrating.

Thank you to Mary Sullivan, who, one evening many, many years ago said, *you need to write poetry.* Such luck to have her hand on my shoulder ever since.

Most of all, to my wife, Debbie, and to my inspiring and convention-free kids, as well as my extended family, thank you for the great depth of your love, not to mention the material.

About the Author

Stephen T Berg describes himself as a disappointed hippy, approximate monk, writer, poet. He was raised in Saskatchewan, spent much of his working life in Alberta and currently lives in Maple Bay on Vancouver Island. With an education and background in agriculture he operated prairie grain elevators and worked as a Weed Inspector for Yellowhead County in Alberta. He studied theology and philosophy at Kings College University in Edmonton, is an Oblate of the Order of St. Benedict and spent 25 years working for Hope Mission, an agency that cares for homeless people. Before his retirement from Hope Mission he authored the book *Growing Hope*, an 80-year history of the Edmonton based organization. In 2009 he was the recipient of the Waldo Ranson *Spirit of Edmonton* Award.

A frequent contributor to the *Edmonton Journal's* Religion page, Stephen wrote articles on social care, justice and environmental stewardship. He also had a column in the Catholic newspaper, *Prairie Messenger*, called *Porch Light*. While a member of ICWF (InScribe Christian Writers' Fellowship), he won awards in both poetry and nonfiction. Sponsored by *Orion Magazine*, he attended Wildbranch Writing Workshop in Vermont, later serving a term as board member for *Orion*. His prose and poetry have appeared in such publications as *Prairie Fire, Orion, Earthshine, Geez, oratorealis,* and Vancouver's *Westender*. His first chapbook, *There Are No Small Moments*, was published by The Rasp and The Wine (2014). In 2016-2017 Stephen earned The Writer's Studio Creative Writing Certificate from Simon Fraser University. For more of his work, visit growmercy.org.

Other Aeolus House Books

Elder Heart by K.D. Miller
The Undead by Colin Morton
The River Doesn't Stop by Ariane Blackman
Fox Haunts by Penn Kemp
Panoptic by Thomas Gannon Hamilton
Poems for the Politically Incontinent by Sydney White
Living Names by Brian Cameron
The Heart of All Music by Stanley Fefferman
Pod and Berry by Allan Briesmaster
Someone Who Watched Over Me by Oonagh Berry
Out of Place by Kate Rogers
Islands North and South by Rosemary Clewes
Visited by Chance by James LaTrobe
What We Will Miss by Roger Bell
River Neither by Allan Briesmaster
What is this thing to feel the world by Jeevan Mykoo
Hard Times by Rob Rolfe
Foreign Skin by Kate Rogers
A Book of Riddlu by John Reibetanz
The Laundress of Time by Donna Langevin
two jammed suitcases by Judith Anderson Stuart
Cry Uncle, ed. by Allan Briesmaster, Sue Chenette and Maureen Hynes
Acting My Age by Linda Stitt
Adder's-tongues by Norma West Linder
Another Way of Falling by Mary Ellen Csamer
Parallel Shores by Tessa Too-Kong
With a Will by Linda Stitt
Arcana by Clara Blackwood
While the Music Lasts by Frank Young
So Rare by Stan Patton
Opening the Stone Heart by James Deahl
Sapphire Seasons by I.B. Iskov
A Dark Clarity by Michael Kirkham
Offerings by Dorothy Sandler-Glick